ISAAC

ISAAC

The Biblical Character Series

WHITELAW

Swackie Ltd

CONTENTS

Introduction		1
1	Birth of Isaac	2
2	Isaac on the Altar	7
3	Isaac's Marriage	13
4	Abraham's Death	17
5	Birth of Jacob & Esau	20
6	Isaac Follows Abraham's Error	22
7	Quarrels with Wells	25
8	Treaty with Abimelech	28
9	Isaac Deceived	31
10	Esau's Anger	35
11	Jacob Sent Away	39
12	Isaac's Death	42

Introduction

Introduction

I firmly believe that every verse in the Bible has meaning for us today in the twenty-first century. If it did not, God would not have let it become part of the Bible. Every verse is there for a purpose, whether for encouragement, correction, guidance, or various reasons.

I love studying Biblical characters, so I started writing this series of books. I think every personality in the Bible is fascinating, simply because they have meaning for us today.

When I studied the character of Abraham, it was clear to me that the story of Abraham was likened to our spiritual walk and represented the steps and stages we would encounter in our lives. When I then turned to Isaac, I puzzled over him for a while, reading and re-reading the account of his life and wondering what the overall significance for us is today?

Then I felt God say to me, "Isaac is like the Church today. He is a great man but achieves little." When God speaks to me like that, it still comes as a shock, but then when I look at it, yes, it's right. The Church is a great organisation, but it is achieving little today.

Therefore, any burdened that the Church is achieving little need to study the character of Isaac and learn from him. This book seeks to recount the life of Isaac and look for deeper meaning related to us in the twenty-first century, but I must confess, I found this a difficult book to write, and I hope this does not detract from the content.

CHAPTER 1

Birth of Isaac

<u>Birth of Isaac</u>
Genesis Ch 21 v 1 – 8
Now the Lord was gracious to Sarah as he had said, and the Lord did for Sarah what he had promised. Sarah became pregnant and bore a son to Abraham in his old age, at the very time God had promised him. Abraham gave the name Isaac to the son Sarah bore him. When his son Isaac was eight days old, Abraham circumcised him, as God commanded him. Abraham was a hundred years old when his son Isaac was born to him.

Sarah said, "God has brought me laughter, and everyone who hears about this will laugh with me." And she added, "Who would have said to Abraham that Sarah would nurse children? Yet I have borne him a son in his old age."

The child grew and was weaned, and on the day Isaac was weaned Abraham held a great feast.

Isaac was the child of promise. Abraham and Sarah were promised a son twenty years before he was born. They had struggled to believe it at first, especially since they were so old, and in their unbelief, they had taken things into their own hands.

Initially, God had told Abraham that he would have a son, but Abraham reasoned that God hadn't said it would be Sarah's son, so he had lain with Sarah's maid, Hagar, and she had conceived and born him a son called Ishmael.

God then clarified his message that the son of promise would be Sarah's son. The practice of having more than one wife would have been widespread at this time, but it was not God's way, and only the first wife would be recognised as a true wife and therefore as being able to produce legitimate offspring.

Having taken matters into their own hands (Sarah was compliant, indeed, led the initiative), they generated a massive problem which is still causing trouble to this day, four thousand years later, between the descendants of Isaac and Ishmael.

So it was that Isaac, although he was the son of promise, was born into strife and trouble from day one. As soon as he was born, there was a crisis between Sarah and Hagar, and Abraham was forced to send Hagar and Ishmael away. This is in verses nine through twenty-one, which we did not read, but you may do well to study these too.

We can well imagine the bitterness harboured by Hagar. She had been a faithful servant for years, and her son had been a comfort to Abraham for around fourteen years. Now they were to be thrown out into the desert to survive on their own as best as they could. We can also imagine how that bitterness would be fermenting inside Hagar and passed on to Ishmael, who would develop a hatred of his half-brother.

Isaac's life was never going to be easy due to this rift in the family, but he would grow up in a very privileged position. Abraham was a wealthy man, and everything he had was to be passed on to Isaac. Isaac would be groomed to take over as the head of the family and would be taught the ways of God from birth, as Abraham saw this as essential.

The name Isaac means laughter, which is entirely appropriate. Laughter was Abraham and Sarah's first response when God told them she would bear a son. She was ninety years old at the time and well beyond the age for carrying children, so laughter was indeed the same response we would likely have had. The reaction did not please God, though, who wanted to build faith in these two who would be the forerunners of God's people.

We would say now that Sarah was laughing on the other side of her face. Indeed, Sarah was overjoyed with her long-awaited son, and he was, no doubt, spoiled and overindulged. The Bible does not say explicitly, but from references later, I think we could assume that Isaac was extremely close to his father and mother and probably did not interact very well with anyone outside his little circle.

Reading through the passages on Isaac, we get the feeling he may have been a bit of an introvert. We do not read of Isaac having much interaction with others throughout his life, which may explain his actions as we study his character further.

There was much joy in the household when Isaac was born, and Abraham held a great feast. We must remember that Abraham's retinue would have extended to many hundreds, possibly well over a thousand. We know Abraham had three hundred and eighteen trained fighting men in his household at least twenty years before this, and we would assume that at least some of the men had wives and children.

Isaac would have been born into a sizeable community where he would have been looked on as the crown prince and may well have been brought up by his mother to stand aloof from the other children in the community, making him a bit of a loner.

The Church, in the world, is something similar. Isaac represents the Church, but Ishmael represents the world, and there is much hostility between the two. It is not surprising since the father of the two bodies is God and Satan. Satan has cultivated hatred in his followers just as Hagar developed hatred in Ishmael.

This division went right back to the garden of Eden when Eve ate the forbidden fruit, and then Adam ate also. This separated all of humanity from God, and a route back to communion with God was only through faith and trust in him. Often, man tries to take matters into his own hands and recreate the way back to God. All have failed and always will fail.

God has clarified his message to us many times and in many ways, but mainly through his scriptures. Just as it did not work out Abraham taking a shortcut, the route to communion with God and eternal residence with him in Heaven is not to be found by taking shortcuts, but by the only way he proscribes, through his Son, Jesus.

As a Church, how long do we wait for revival? There are plenty of places in the Bible where it is promised, just as Abraham and Sarah were promised a son, but it does not appear until the time is right and we must wait. Faith also has much to do with it; you see, Abraham and Sarah took quite a long time to believe that God could do this. When they did agree that God could do it, they still thought there would be a trick involved and that it would be through Sarah's maid, not Sarah herself. They were still holding on to their unbelief, and the Son did not come until they took God seriously and believed his promise. Revival will be the same.

The Church will always face strife and trouble from the unbelieving world. The world is bitter and hates us because, deep down, they know that they do not have what we have. They do not want what we have, but they would like to take it away from us also.

Our life as Christians is never going to be easy, but we will grow up in a privileged position like Isaac. All that our Heavenly Father has is ours. We are sons, heirs, joint-heirs with Jesus of every good thing the Father possesses.

Just as when Isaac was born, there is much joy in Heaven whenever a new soul is added to the local Church. The Church is privileged, and the riches available to us as heirs to the Kingdom are beyond description.

These riches, however, are only available to legitimate heirs, and anyone claiming to have come another way, except through Jesus, has no part in the inheritance.

Just as Hagar and Ishmael were sent away, anyone not of true faith must also be sent away from fellowship. The world does not understand this and hates us for this. There is a bitterness in the world against the Church which will never diminish.

Just as the Church in Acts chapter two was born in miraculous events, any fresh revival of faith will also be birthed in a supernatural experience. God can work his wonders to make a nation from dry bones, and he can revive a Church from dead spiritual dry worship.

One of the Churches' most significant problems, especially as they mature and start to drift from the faith, is that they become introverted. They do not mix with the world in any way and cannot reach the world with the Gospel. When Jesus walked this earth, he walked among the people, talked to them, listened to them, and healed them. We are called to do the same. Cutting ourselves off from the world is not the answer.

CHAPTER 2

Isaac on the Altar

<u>Isaac on the Altar</u>
Genesis Ch 22 v 1 – 14
Some time later God tested Abraham. He said to him, "Abraham!"
"Here I am," he replied.
Then God said, "Take your son, your only son, whom you love—Isaac—and go to the region of Moriah. Sacrifice him there as a burnt offering on a mountain I will show you."
Early the next morning Abraham got up and loaded his donkey. He took with him two of his servants and his son Isaac. When he had cut enough wood for the burnt offering, he set out for the place God had told him about. On the third day Abraham looked up and saw the place in the distance. He said to his servants, "Stay here with the donkey while I and the boy go over there. We will worship and then we will come back to you."
Abraham took the wood for the burnt offering and placed it on his son Isaac, and he himself carried the fire and the knife. As the two of them went on together, Isaac spoke up and said to his father Abraham, "Father?"
"Yes, my son?" Abraham replied.

"The fire and wood are here," Isaac said, "but where is the lamb for the burnt offering?"

Abraham answered, "God himself will provide the lamb for the burnt offering, my son." And the two of them went on together.

When they reached the place God had told him about, Abraham built an altar there and arranged the wood on it. He bound his son Isaac and laid him on the altar, on top of the wood. Then he reached out his hand and took the knife to slay his son. But the angel of the Lord called out to him from Heaven, "Abraham! Abraham!"

"Here I am," he replied.

"Do not lay a hand on the boy," he said. "Do not do anything to him. Now I know that you fear God, because you have not withheld from me your son, your only son."

Abraham looked up and there in a thicket he saw a ram caught by its horns. He went over and took the ram and sacrificed it as a burnt offering instead of his son. So Abraham called that place The Lord Will Provide. And to this day it is said, "On the mountain of the Lord it will be provided."

This is a difficult passage for us to study and understand. It raises some highly uncomfortable questions about why God would ask this of Abraham. It also causes us to consider what Isaac thought of this while it was happening.

Reading between the lines, I think we can assume that Abraham and Sarah were delighted with their long-awaited son and spoiled and pampered him in every way. As is the way of mothers, Sarah most likely wrapped him in cotton wool. I think we could conclude that Abraham and Sarah loved their son above everything else, and probably their lives revolved around him.

God knows our every being, every fibre of our body, mind and spirit and did not need to put Abraham through this test to know that Abraham would be faithful and carry out any request God made. So why did God ask Abraham to do this?

We need to go to the book of Job to answer this question. Many events are going on behind the scenes in spiritual realms, about which we know nothing. This is clearly described in Job. Although God knew that Job was blameless and upright, even confessing that there was none like him in all the earth, God still allowed the persecution of Job.

I feel we are looking at a similar situation here. God knew Abraham's heart and was convinced that Abraham would be faithful, but there was much more at stake here. Abraham was the father of God's people and the father of the faithful. In years, centuries and even four thousand years later, God's people are going to look back and study Abraham. What do they see? A man who granted every advantage but none of the tests we endure? No! It was essential God's people could look back at Abraham and see an example to follow.

We need to understand that God was building his people, and the foundations had to be strong. The descendants of Abraham had to be able to look back and see where they had come from and realise that they came from the strongest and best example of a man that ever lived. Of course, they had to admit that Abraham was a man, just like themselves, and accept that he made mistakes, just as they did, but the overall picture had to be a man close to God who lived a life worth imitating.

Where does that leave Isaac? I feel that Isaac probably idolised his father and mother. I think he most likely had little or no contact with the outside world, and his family was his entire existence. It would seem that Abraham told no one what he was about to do. Only he and Isaac went on the final leg of the journey, and it is clear he had not told Isaac, as Isaac even noticed that the sacrifice was missing.

Isaac was used to sacrifices, which is no surprise since Abraham built an altar wherever he went to worship God and sacrifice to him. This must have been an adventure to Isaac, journeying away from his mother, perhaps for the first time in his life. As they make the last few miles, Isaac is puzzled and asks Abraham where the lamb for the burnt offering is?

I often wonder what went through Isaac's mind as they reached the place appointed and Abraham starts building his altar. Then Abraham takes the wood and places it on top of the altar, ready for the sacrifice. Isaac must have been waiting eagerly for God to provide a sacrifice.

What happened after this? Did Abraham sit down and explain to Isaac what was to happen, or did he get on with it without explanation? The next verse simply tells us Abraham bound Isaac and laid him on the altar. It would seem to suggest that he was not going on the altar willingly if Isaac needed to be restrained. Then again, we do not read of any objection by Isaac, and his entire life, he does seem always to be compliant and accommodating.

This is a very solemn moment in history which is a parallel with the day Jesus went to the cross to be the ultimate sacrifice. Isaac was to be spared, but no substitute was found for Jesus as there was no alternative if we were to be saved. Notably, the spot where Isaac was to be offered was very close to where Jesus would be sacrificed two thousand years later.

I can't help but notice this period of two thousand years. It was around two thousand years since creation, then another two thousand until Jesus died, and now another two thousand years are almost complete. There is a pattern emerging here, and this is another pointer that we are very close to the end of days and the second coming of our saviour.

Child sacrifice was certainly not God's ways, and in many places in scripture, God is very clear that he despises this practice. This was quite simply a test that was never going to be carried out, and as predicted by Abraham, God provided the sacrifice.

There is no record of Isaac's reaction to this episode, which is a great pity. We are left wondering if this was responsible for the natural tendency for Isaac to shy away from trouble his entire life.

We are not going to read the record of Sarah's death in chapter twenty-three of Genesis. Although we know from other sources that her death affected Isaac greatly, he is not mentioned in the chapter. Sarah was one hundred and twenty-seven years old when she died, so we would estimate that Isaac would have been around thirty-five years old at this point. If Isaac was so disturbed by his mother's passing, it reinforces the idea that Isaac was overly attached to his mother.

When God moves in revival, the Church is unstoppable and is like a river in full flow. The experience, I would imagine, is like nothing else we have ever experienced. The Church is on a mountaintop and soaring like the birds. Of course, this never lasts, and after a period of vitality, the Church will always find itself under pressure. Every revival has been the same and always will be.

The world takes a little while to catch on that something is happening, but it always wants to stamp it out when it does. Ironically, it is usually an organised religion that plays this part as they feel threatened. It is always only a matter of time before the Church is placed on the altar. It is not a pleasant thing, nor a pleasant place, but all new Christians and Churches need to go through to establish and grow our faith.

God does not want us to go through these trials, but there is no other way to prove our faith. Just as gold must go through the fire to purify it, so must we as Christians must be purified. God is building a people. He doesn't want wishy-washy people; he wants strong people to shine their light into a dark world.

When we are on the altar, we may well feel abandoned and confused, but if you are going through this, look to Jesus, who has gone this road before. Let him be your example and renew your faith in God, who you know already can do all things.

Remember, earlier; I talked about two thousand years. I firmly believe that we are approaching the very end days, and you will undoubtedly be hated more by the world as the end draws nearer. Satan knows his time is drawing to a close, and he is angry and will lash out as much as he can. The Bible tells us things will continue to worsen, so do not despair. It is all part of God's plan.

CHAPTER 3

Isaac's Marriage

<u>Isaac's Marriage</u>
Genesis Ch 24 v 1 – 9 & v 61 – 67
Abraham was now very old, and the Lord had blessed him in every way. He said to the senior servant in his household, the one in charge of all that he had, "Put your hand under my thigh. I want you to swear by the Lord, the God of Heaven and the God of earth, that you will not get a wife for my son from the daughters of the Canaanites, among whom I am living, but will go to my country and my own relatives and get a wife for my son Isaac."

The servant asked him, "What if the woman is unwilling to come back with me to this land? Shall I then take your son back to the country you came from?"

"Make sure that you do not take my son back there," Abraham said. "The Lord, the God of Heaven, who brought me out of my father's household and my native land and who spoke to me and promised me on oath, saying, 'To your offspring I will give this land'—he will send his angel before you so that you can get a wife for my son from there. If the woman is unwilling to come back with you, then you will be released from this oath of

mine. Only do not take my son back there." So the servant put his hand under the thigh of his master Abraham and swore an oath to him concerning this matter.

Then Rebekah and her attendants got ready and mounted the camels and went back with the man. So the servant took Rebekah and left.

Now Isaac had come from Beer Lahai Roi, for he was living in the Negev. He went out to the field one evening to meditate, and as he looked up, he saw camels approaching. Rebekah also looked up and saw Isaac. She got down from her camel and asked the servant, "Who is that man in the field coming to meet us?"

"He is my master," the servant answered. So she took her veil and covered herself.

Then the servant told Isaac all he had done. Isaac brought her into the tent of his mother Sarah, and he married Rebekah. So she became his wife, and he loved her; and Isaac was comforted after his mother's death.

We have not read the entire chapter, but I urge you to read it as it is a beautiful love story in action. Isaac was the line in which the promise would extend, and the line needed to be pure, and God had already made it clear that it was hazardous to the faith to be aligned with the godless tribes around them. The only answer was to find a wife for Isaac from his relatives.

As Abraham remembered when he went down into Egypt, he did not want Isaac to leave this land for the fear that he may settle elsewhere and not return. Abraham discussed this with his closest servant, and it would seem a probability that it was not even discussed with Isaac.

Abraham seems very agitated at the possibility that Isaac should leave the land and settle elsewhere and instructs the servant, on no account, to take Isaac back to their former abode. It may also have been a case that Isaac missed his mother so much that he could not be parted from his father, but in any case, Abraham decided to send his servant to find a wife for Isaac.

This account shows us once again that Isaac was passive and compliant, happy to accept a wife which he did not choose, and he doesn't even seem to have sought any input into the choice.

The servant finds a wife, who is reported to be extremely beautiful, who is the daughter of Isaac's first cousin, and she agrees to accompany the servant back to marry Isaac. There were no photographs in those days, so Rebekah would not have known what Isaac looked like and only known what the servant told her.

They would, no doubt, already have heard that Abraham was very successful and prosperous. This would have been confirmed by the servant bestowing many gifts on the family, especially on Rebekah. Would this have had any bearing on Rebekah's decision to accept the proposal?

Rebekah agrees with the proposal and is eager to set off to her new life. Arriving in Canaan, Isaac is delighted and takes Rebekah as his wife and loves her. However, nowhere in the narrative does it ever say Rebekah loved Isaac. It would seem that Rebekah carried out her duties as a wife but that it was more a marriage of convenience for her. We will see more evidence to back this up as we continue our study.

As believers, our life's partner must be a believer. Any alliance with unbelievers will render us impotent and of no use in God's kingdom. Our young people must think seriously before choosing a lifelong partner and ask the question, what is the benefit of this alliance be to the Kingdom?

Christ went to the cross for us, gave his life for us, and we must be willing to offer our lives as a living sacrifice for him. Any other outcome is an act of unfaithfulness to the one who loved us enough to die for us.

Young people must also look to God in these matters and trust that God has the ideal partner looked out for them. Just as God had looked out Rebekah for Isaac, God will provide the correct person to partner us in the remainder of our lives.

Similarly, as a Church, we must be careful with whom we associate. There is a movement these days towards ecumenical worship, but those who do not have the same fundamental beliefs have no place worshipping God with us. Some in the Christian Church even go as far as to appease Muslims, who are the descendants of Ishmael. These people oppose and deny Christ and can have no part with us. This will not end in converting them but in us compromising.

The Church must remain pure and not compromise with the world. We certainly need to be in the world and interact with it; otherwise, we cannot reach the lost, but we must not become like the world. If we become like the world, we have nothing different to offer them.

Like Isaac, we do need to be passive when God is leading. If the spirit of God is leading us in a new direction, we need to be receptive to the leading while still testing that it is the Holy Spirit leading and not an evil spirit. We need to be especially careful who we partner with, and communication with God on this subject is required. As in Isaac's case, God will always look out for the best for us.

One other point to note here is that as the Church is in full flow, it has a richness that will attract people. All who come to Church may not be there as true believers. Some may be there for other reasons, for what they can get out of it and status.

CHAPTER 4

Abraham's Death

Abraham's Death
Genesis Ch 25 v 1 – 11

Abraham had taken another wife, whose name was Keturah. She bore him Zimran, Jokshan, Medan, Midian, Ishbak and Shuah. Jokshan was the father of Sheba and Dedan; the descendants of Dedan were the Ashurites, the Letushites and the Leummites. The sons of Midian were Ephah, Epher, Hanok, Abida and Eldaah. All these were descendants of Keturah.

Abraham left everything he owned to Isaac. But while he was still living, he gave gifts to the sons of his concubines and sent them away from his son Isaac to the land of the east.

Abraham lived a hundred and seventy-five years. Then Abraham breathed his last and died at a good old age, an old man and full of years; and he was gathered to his people. His sons Isaac and Ishmael buried him in the cave of Machpelah near Mamre, in the field of Ephron son of Zohar the Hittite, the field Abraham had bought from the Hittites. There Abraham was buried with his wife Sarah. After Abraham's death, God blessed his son Isaac, who then lived near Beer Lahai Roi.

Studying the character of Isaac, we often have to rely on what is unsaid rather than what is written. My conclusions may be wrong, but I put together a narrative based on what seems most logical. This has made this the most challenging book I have written so far.

Very little seems to have been stated about any interaction between Isaac and Abraham after Isaac's marriage. I think we are looking at a significant shift in Isaac's focus here. He was previously focused on his father and mother, but his full attention is now taken up by his wife, Rebekah.

This is precisely what it should be, but I do sense that it is a little more than just a change of focus and perhaps more of an estrangement. As I have said before, Isaac seems to be easily led and manipulated by whoever he happens to trust at the time, and it is a blessing that no harm came to him. From the point of his marriage, Rebekah seems to direct his paths. Maybe, today, we would say Rebekah wore the trousers in this family.

On top of this, Abraham has also taken a new wife and had a new family, which Isaac or Rebekah may not have very enthusiastically received. Isaac seems to have moved away from Abraham's area and has settled elsewhere.

It is interesting to note that both Isaac and Ishmael are present to bury him when Abraham died. I would imagine that it would have been one of those strained meetings. Abraham was buried alongside Sarah in the cave he had bought and was his only possession in the land.

After the death of Abraham, God blessed Isaac, but it was for Abraham's sake, rather than Isaacs. Isaac was a Godly man, but he just did not take it, or anything else he did, to excess. God also blessed Ishmael, and the two half-brothers did continue to live nearby for some time.

Just as Abraham gave all that he had to Isaac, God provides all he has to us. We may well, just like Isaac, not be entirely focussed on God, but you can be sure God is wholly focussed on us. Just as Abraham sent away every person who could be a problem to Isaac, so God protects and provides for us. God loves us, just as Abraham loved Isaac.

If a Church starts to interact with another partner and places more trust in the partner than in God, then the Church's focus will change dramatically. The interaction and communication with God will continually recede from importance, and we will be relying on another source to guide us. It should not be necessary to tell readers that this is a dangerous position and will result in complete estrangement from God.

The Church will then find itself in the same place as Isaac, being ruled and manipulated by a partner who has ulterior motives and adverse to any other relationship. We have seen this many times when certain Church sections will not have any dealings with God's children in other Churches. The Brethren were particularly prone to this, and some would not even have a meal with a believer from another Church.

If we adopt this position where we will not even relate to our brothers and sisters in the Lord, how can we ever hope to connect to the lost world around us? Jesus shared a meal with the lowest of sinners, and we should be prepared to do the same.

CHAPTER 5

Birth of Jacob & Esau

Birth of Jacob & Esau
Genesis Ch 25 v 19 – 24

This is the account of the family line of Abraham's son Isaac.

Abraham became the father of Isaac, and Isaac was forty years old when he married Rebekah daughter of Bethuel the Aramean from Paddan Aram and sister of Laban the Aramean.

Isaac prayed to the Lord on behalf of his wife, because she was childless. The Lord answered his prayer, and his wife Rebekah became pregnant. The babies jostled each other within her, and she said, "Why is this happening to me?" So she went to inquire of the Lord.

The Lord said to her, "Two nations are in your womb, and two peoples from within you will be separated; one people will be stronger than the other, and the older will serve the younger."

When the time came for her to give birth, there were twin boys in her womb. The first to come out was red, and his whole body was like a hairy garment; so they named him Esau. After this, his brother came out, with his hand grasping Esau's heel; so he was named Jacob. Isaac was sixty years old when Rebekah gave birth to them.

It is clear from this passage that Isaac and Rebekah had an ongoing relationship with God. Both go to God for answers when they have a problem. However, unlike his father, we rarely hear of Isaac building altars and worshipping God. His relationship with God seems to be more a case of going through the motions.

Firstly, Isaac prayed on behalf of Rebekah as she could not have children. Contrast this with Rebekah praying for herself. This seems to sum up the relationship between the two of them. Isaac was selfless, but Rebekah was self-centred. Rebekah only goes to God when she has a problem.

God answers Rebekah quite comprehensively, advising her that she is having twins and forming two nations and that the younger child shall be the dominant one. When the two children are born, they are entirely different, which they would continue to be throughout their entire existence.

Like Isaac and Rebekah, our Church is becoming a dysfunctional family. The fellowship still proceeds, but in general, prayer is restricted to times when we need something or it is a dry affair. There is no sense of being put on an altar at this point, and the Church is starting to be seen as something which protects you from trouble or persecution. There can also be a feeling that you pray for anything you wish, and it is your right to receive it.

Those growing up in the faith within these Churches, like Esau and Jacob, come in two different types. I can relate to this as I grew up in a Church in this position. While I have continued in the faith, many others, probably the majority, have rejected the faith as what they were taught and what they saw simply did not match up.

When it reaches this point in its existence, a Church is much like Isaac, a great institution but accomplishing very little. Growing up within this institution, because it is no longer a Church, members are perplexed and struggle to figure out what it is all about or true.

CHAPTER 6

Isaac Follows Abraham's Error

Isaac Follows Abraham's Error
Genesis Ch 26 v 1 – 11

Now there was a famine in the land—besides the previous famine in Abraham's time—and Isaac went to Abimelek king of the Philistines in Gerar. The Lord appeared to Isaac and said, "Do not go down to Egypt; live in the land where I tell you to live. Stay in this land for a while, and I will be with you and will bless you. For to you and your descendants I will give all these lands and will confirm the oath I swore to your father Abraham. I will make your descendants as numerous as the stars in the sky and will give them all these lands, and through your offspring all nations on earth will be blessed, because Abraham obeyed me and did everything I required of him, keeping my commands, my decrees and my instructions." So Isaac stayed in Gerar.

When the men of that place asked him about his wife, he said, "She is my sister," because he was afraid to say, "She is my wife." He thought, "The men of this place might kill me on account of Rebekah, because she is beautiful."

When Isaac had been there a long time, Abimelek king of the Philistines looked down from a window and saw Isaac caressing his wife Rebekah. So Abimelek summoned Isaac and said, "She is really your wife! Why did you say, 'She is my sister'?"

Isaac answered him, "Because I thought I might lose my life on account of her."

Then Abimelek said, "What is this you have done to us? One of the men might well have slept with your wife, and you would have brought guilt upon us."

So Abimelek gave orders to all the people: "Anyone who harms this man or his wife shall surely be put to death."

Here we see a repeat of Abraham's situation when he first arrived in Canaan around seventy years previously. Isaac makes the same mistake that Abraham made and pretends that Rebekah is his sister when he moves to Gerar. Gerar was the same place and the same King as Abraham had made the same mistake before Isaac had been born.

King Abimelech finally finds out the truth just as he had done with Abraham, but he does not throw Isaac out this time. Isaac is allowed to remain, and the king warns all his people against taking action against Isaac or Rebekah.

If we look back through the Church's history, we will see example after example of this same error. A movement of God starts up a new branch of the Church and sees great results. We can look back at the reformation, the covenanters, the Methodists, the Brethren movement, the Charismatic movement and many more.

Each was born out of frustration of a Church that had grown into a system. A Church which had gone down into Egypt. A Church that was aligning with the world rather than remaining faithful to God's will.

Isaac repeated the same error as his father, and churches repeat the same mistake as previous Churches. Churches start on fire and with Pentecostal growth. When the two types of people come into the Church, it causes problems, so rules are applied. Over time, the rules become more important than the spirit that enabled the Church. The Spirit is quenched, and the system takes over control. The Church continues but slowly loses the fire and passion and becomes lifeless. A new frustration builds up in the true believers, and the cycle starts all over again with a new Church.

How do we stop our Church from going down into Egypt? Stay close to God. God is not in Egypt. If we consult and consider God in everything we do as a Church, we will not go down into Egypt. Of course, that is not always easy, as Satan goes about like a roaring lion, seeking to destroy the Church.

There are tremendous pressures on the Church to update and modernise. While the Church does need to do this, it must also examine all things new to see if they are from God or a distraction sent from the father of lies. We must also explore the benefits of any new ideas to the Church. It is not an answer that it will attract a particular personality to the Church.

An excellent example of this is the movement towards modern music in the Church. Some of the new music have great words, some have great music, and some have both. The question I like to ask, what is the purpose of it. Music within the Church is predominantly about worship. If a new song is not the type you can sing along to, it is not worship. It is entertainment. Nothing is wrong with that in its place, but if we come to Church to worship and face songs we cannot sing, then we cannot worship God. We are being entertained.

CHAPTER 7

Quarrels with Wells

<u>Quarrels with Wells</u>
Genesis Ch 26 v 12 – 22
Isaac planted crops in that land and the same year reaped a hundredfold, because the Lord blessed him. The man became rich, and his wealth continued to grow until he became very wealthy. He had so many flocks and herds and servants that the Philistines envied him. So all the wells that his father's servants had dug in the time of his father Abraham, the Philistines stopped up, filling them with earth.

Then Abimelek said to Isaac, "Move away from us; you have become too powerful for us."

So Isaac moved away from there and encamped in the Valley of Gerar, where he settled. Isaac reopened the wells that had been dug in the time of his father Abraham, which the Philistines had stopped up after Abraham died, and he gave them the same names his father had given them.

Isaac's servants dug in the valley and discovered a well of fresh water there. But the herders of Gerar quarreled with those of Isaac and said, "The water is ours!" So he named the well Esek, because they disputed with him. Then they dug another well, but they quarreled over that one also; so he named it Sitnah. He moved on from there and dug another well, and no one quarreled over it. He named it Rehoboth, saying, "Now the Lord has given us room and we will flourish in the land."

Why would the Philistines fill in the wells Abraham had dug? They were envious. They were not successful, and they simply did not want Abraham or Isaac to be successful either. If we are successful as a Church, expect the world to be angry.

Isaac planted crops and reaped one hundred-fold that same year. We, as a Church, need to sow seed. We need to water the seed with our prayers. Take note here, the one thing the enemy wants to stop is the watering of the crops, which is symbolic of prayer. Above all other things, Satan would wish to prevent us from praying. He knows how powerful prayer is, even if we do not. He will stop prayer if possible.

Interestingly, the Philistines did not try to stop Isaac from planting seed. Similarly, Satan will not attempt to stop us from planting seed at first. His focus is on ensuring the seed does not grow. He knows he cannot prevent the planting of the seed. If Churches do not plant it, it will be planted from elsewhere. Just like when Jesus came into Jerusalem triumphant, he said if the people did not cry out, then the stones would. Similarly, the seed of the Gospel will be planted, but Satan is determined to stop the seed from growing.

Look around you at the Churches in your area. Many no longer have prayer meetings as no one will attend. Satan does not bother these Churches. They are no threat to him. They will not be stealing souls from him. We must be ever vigilant to protect and continue our prayer meeting. When we give up on prayer, we would be as well close the door to the Church. The prayer meeting is the engine of the Church. If there is no engine, there is no progress.

Every time that Isaac dug a well, the unbelievers quarrelled with him over the well. He had to move on and dig a new well. Note here the big difference between Isaac and his father, Abraham. Isaac dug wells first, but Abraham built altars and worshipped God first. We, as a Church, must dig wells and water our seed, but we must not forget to place our lives on the altar and worship and thank God for every good blessing he has bestowed on us.

So many times, Isaac was hassled and had to move on. As the Church, we will be no different, and we will face opposition in everything we do. The world will try to stop us from praying, but they will dispute with us over our successes when they cannot do that. Everything we do, as a Church, will be contested. Note that they even try to stop us preaching in the times we live in now.

Churches have been closed during this pandemic, and even when pubs and restaurants can open back up, Churches still have restrictions. Pastors preaching in the street are now routinely arrested on the slightest pretence. Churches and Christian teachers are no longer allowed to teach the gospel message in schools. They are even now trying to pass legislation that prevents Churches praying for homosexuals to be delivered from bondage.

The world is pressing around us in the entire western world, and Christians should not be surprised if we soon find ourselves a persecuted minority. Indeed, the likelihood of this is so strong; we should now be preparing our congregation for this to happen.

<u>Note also how Isaac views his position here. He finishes up with the declaration, "Now the Lord has given us room and we will flourish in the land". It is critical to note that Isaac declares **WE** will flourish, not the Lord will make us flourish. Isaac is wholly dependent on his own abilities and does not acknowledge that God has blessed him.</u>

CHAPTER 8

Treaty with Abimelech

Treaty with Abimelech
Genesis Ch 26 v 23 – 35

From there he went up to Beersheba. That night the Lord appeared to him and said, "I am the God of your father Abraham. Do not be afraid, for I am with you; I will bless you and will increase the number of your descendants for the sake of my servant Abraham."

Isaac built an altar there and called on the name of the Lord. There he pitched his tent, and there his servants dug a well.

Meanwhile, Abimelek had come to him from Gerar, with Ahuzzath his personal adviser and Phicol the commander of his forces. Isaac asked them, "Why have you come to me, since you were hostile to me and sent me away?"

They answered, "We saw clearly that the Lord was with you; so we said, 'There ought to be a sworn agreement between us'—between us and you. Let us make a treaty with you that you will do us no harm, just as we did not harm you but always treated you well and sent you away peacefully. And now you are blessed by the Lord."

Isaac then made a feast for them, and they ate and drank. Early the next morning the men swore an oath to each other. Then Isaac sent them on their way, and they went away peacefully.

That day Isaac's servants came and told him about the well they had dug. They said, "We've found water!" He called it Shibah, and to this day the name of the town has been Beersheba.

When Esau was forty years old, he married Judith daughter of Beeri the Hittite, and also Basemath daughter of Elon the Hittite. They were a source of grief to Isaac and Rebekah.

Ah! At last! Isaac builds an altar. There is nothing like persecution and trouble to make us run to God. The unbelievers around Isaac have tried everything within their power to bring him down to their level. Despite their best efforts, Isaac has prospered even more. They try a different approach. They come to make peace with Isaac but bring the commander of their forces with them. Isaac had never quarrelled with them in any way, so why would they need to bring their commander with them?

They bring him to intimidate Isaac. They admit that they can see that the Lord is with Isaac and want to make peace with him. They want him to enter a treaty. Isaac is weak and agrees to a treaty. He wines and dines them, and the following day they swore an oath to each other.

I firmly believe this is the point it all goes wrong in Isaac's life. Isaac has taught his children the opposite of what they now see happening in their father's life. They see Isaac making a treaty with the Philistines, so Esau reckons it is also OK for him to take a wife from the tribes around, and indeed, he takes two, which are a source of grief to his parents.

The Bible tells us to swear no oath to any man. We cannot enter into any agreement or treaty with unbelievers. The answer would be to point out to them God's ways and advise them to accept his ways as this is from where our success comes. They can have the same benefits and success as us if they only accept God's ways. We need to explain that we cannot sign a treaty as we cannot give them success, only God can do that, so they need to accept God, not us.

Sadly, Isaac has forgotten about his altar and is now back to digging wells as his main priority. He names this latest well Beersheba, which means "The well of the oath." Isaac is trusting more on the oath with these unbelievers than trusting in God.

As a Church, we must be cautious where we place our trust. Our trust must be in God alone. We cannot put our faith in the ways of the world. We cannot place our confidence on the wells we dig. Our attention must always be focused on the altar.

Isaac Deceived

CHAPTER 9

Isaac Deceived

Genesis Ch 27 v 1 – 29

When Isaac was old and his eyes were so weak that he could no longer see, he called for Esau his older son and said to him, "My son."

"Here I am," he answered.

Isaac said, "I am now an old man and don't know the day of my death. Now then, get your equipment—your quiver and bow—and go out to the open country to hunt some wild game for me. Prepare me the kind of tasty food I like and bring it to me to eat, so that I may give you my blessing before I die."

Now Rebekah was listening as Isaac spoke to his son Esau. When Esau left for the open country to hunt game and bring it back, Rebekah said to her son Jacob, "Look, I overheard your father say to your brother Esau, 'Bring me some game and prepare me some tasty food to eat, so that I may give you my blessing in the presence of the Lord before I die.' Now, my son, listen carefully and do what I tell you: Go out to the flock and bring me two choice young goats, so I can prepare some tasty food for your father, just the way he likes it. Then take it to your father to eat, so that he may give you his blessing before he dies."

Jacob said to Rebekah his mother, "But my brother Esau is a hairy man while I have smooth skin. What if my father touches me? I would appear to be tricking him and would bring down a curse on myself rather than a blessing."

His mother said to him, "My son, let the curse fall on me. Just do what I say; go and get them for me."

So he went and got them and brought them to his mother, and she prepared some tasty food, just the way his father liked it. Then Rebekah took the best clothes of Esau her older son, which she had in the house, and put them on her younger son Jacob. She also covered his hands and the smooth part of his neck with the goatskins. Then she handed to her son Jacob the tasty food and the bread she had made.

He went to his father and said, "My father."

"Yes, my son," he answered. "Who is it?"

Jacob said to his father, "I am Esau your firstborn. I have done as you told me. Please sit up and eat some of my game, so that you may give me your blessing."

Isaac asked his son, "How did you find it so quickly, my son?"

"The Lord your God gave me success," he replied.

Then Isaac said to Jacob, "Come near so I can touch you, my son, to know whether you really are my son Esau or not."

Jacob went close to his father Isaac, who touched him and said, "The voice is the voice of Jacob, but the hands are the hands of Esau." He did not recognise him, for his hands were hairy like those of his brother Esau; so he proceeded to bless him. "Are you really my son Esau?" he asked.

"I am," he replied.

Then he said, "My son, bring me some of your game to eat, so that I may give you my blessing."

Jacob brought it to him and he ate; and he brought some wine and he drank. Then his father Isaac said to him, "Come here, my son, and kiss me."

So he went to him and kissed him. When Isaac caught the smell of his clothes, he blessed him and said,

"Ah, the smell of my son is like the smell of a field that the Lord has blessed. May God give you Heaven's dew and earth's richness— an abundance of grain and new wine. May nations serve you and peoples bow down to you. Be Lord over your brothers, and may the sons of your mother bow down to you. May those who curse you be cursed and those who bless you be blessed."

Oh! What a tale of deception. When we thought that Isaac and Rebekah had a perfect marriage, here we see Rebekah plotting behind Isaac's back to trick him into blessing her favourite. Meanwhile, Isaac seems to be more interested in what's in it for him. He is happy to bless his eldest son, but at the same time, he has an eye for what he is going to get out of it.

How many Churches do we see like this? Old and blind and easily deceived. Churches hanker after the things of the world and unaware of when our partners are plotting against us.

Rebekah shows her true colours here and plots with Jacob to steal the ultimate prize, the father's blessing. They conspire to deceive Isaac and carry it off successfully.

Look at the Churches in our land these days. Members come into the Church who look and feel like believers, but their voice is different. Churches are filled with people like this. They act like believers but talk about another gospel that is different to that which Jesus gave us.

The Churches are easily deceived as they are old and blind. They do not seek the counsel of God but listen to the lies they are told and accept them. The Churches are faced with many conspiracies and falsehoods, and we should always be on our guard against such.

Here, we see that Rebekah was manipulating and had no problem deceiving her husband. There is no love on Rebekah's part as Isaac had loved her.

This part of the story is very much applicable today as this is precisely where the vast majority of our Churches are today. Most Churches are now totally dysfunctional and irrelevant to the world around us. They are shining no light into an ever-darkening world. They are as blind as the world around them.

CHAPTER 10

Esau's Anger

<u>Esau's Anger</u>
Genesis Ch 27 v 30 – 46

After Isaac finished blessing him, and Jacob had scarcely left his father's presence, his brother Esau came in from hunting. He too prepared some tasty food and brought it to his father. Then he said to him, "My father, please sit up and eat some of my game, so that you may give me your blessing."

His father Isaac asked him, "Who are you?"

"I am your son," he answered, "your firstborn, Esau."

Isaac trembled violently and said, "Who was it, then, that hunted game and brought it to me? I ate it just before you came and I blessed him—and indeed he will be blessed!"

When Esau heard his father's words, he burst out with a loud and bitter cry and said to his father, "Bless me—me too, my father!"

But he said, "Your brother came deceitfully and took your blessing."

Esau said, "Isn't he rightly named Jacob? This is the second time he has taken advantage of me: He took my birthright, and now he's taken my blessing!" Then he asked, "Haven't you reserved any blessing for me?"

Isaac answered Esau, "I have made him Lord over you and have made all his relatives his servants, and I have sustained him with grain and new wine. So what can I possibly do for you, my son?"

Esau said to his father, "Do you have only one blessing, my father? Bless me too, my father!" Then Esau wept aloud.

His father Isaac answered him, "Your dwelling will be away from the earth's richness, away from the dew of Heaven above. You will live by the sword and you will serve your brother. But when you grow restless, you will throw his yoke from off your neck."

Esau held a grudge against Jacob because of the blessing his father had given him. He said to himself, "The days of mourning for my father are near; then I will kill my brother Jacob."

When Rebekah was told what her older son Esau had said, she sent for her younger son Jacob and said to him, "Your brother Esau is planning to avenge himself by killing you. Now then, my son, do what I say: Flee at once to my brother Laban in Harran. Stay with him for a while until your brother's fury subsides. When your brother is no longer angry with you and forgets what you did to him, I'll send word for you to come back from there. Why should I lose both of you in one day?"

Then Rebekah said to Isaac, "I'm disgusted with living because of these Hittite women. If Jacob takes a wife from among the women of this land, from Hittite women like these, my life will not be worth living."

The family just split apart, and there is no longer any pretence. They are divided into two warring camps. One wants to kill the other, while the other simply wants to bend everyone to their advantage and use them to their benefit.

Isaac has pretty much lost interest and is waiting to die. He seems to have given up guiding and instructing his family, and they are doing whatever they think is right. An utterly dysfunctional family, held together by the thinnest of threads.

It is sad when we see this in churches, but even the most successful Churches have this problem. Indeed, it does not happen in a Church that is not successful, as Satan does not bother them and need not cause any trouble there.

What were all the tribes around Isaac and Rebekah thinking now? They must have been watching on with unbelief in what they were seeing, and it is the same when these troubles arise in Churches. The world looks on and gloats.

We do not get to this situation overnight, as to reach this dreadful situation; something has been wrong for an exceedingly long time. Trouble has been fermenting under the surface, and we have not taken care of it, have not asked for God's direction in the matter and have certainly not displayed the grace of God in our relationship with our brothers and sisters.

The story we read here, we know very well, having heard it, and read it many times over the years. However, stop for a minute and consider what you are reading. Consider the deception and the characters involved. It is almost unbelievable to us that Rebekah and Jacob could do this thing, yet it is all part of God's plan.

Alas, even in Churches, we see this level of deception and backstabbing, and we would sometimes ask how believers act this way. As the Apostle James said in James 3:10, "Out of the same mouth come praise and cursing. My brothers and sisters, this should not be."

When we reach this stage, it is never going to end well. There is no easy way out of it when one party intends to kill the other. We may well sympathise with Jacob. After all, God had ordained him to get these things. He was to be the one through which the promise would be continued, but it is the same old story as his father and grandfather, taking things into his own hands and making a right mess of it.

When these things happen in churches, both parties will convince you they are in the right of things, but the simple truth is when it reaches this stage, neither party is acting correctly, and neither party is prepared to turn the other cheek. Where do we go from here, and what happens next?

Even at this stage, we see Rebekah still trying to manipulate everything and still deceiving her husband. It may well be a good idea to send Jacob away, but she plays on Isaac's weaknesses and fears to get her way.

CHAPTER 11

Jacob Sent Away

Jacob Sent Away
Genesis Ch 28 v 1 – 9

So Isaac called for Jacob and blessed him. Then he commanded him: "Do not marry a Canaanite woman. Go at once to Paddan Aram, to the house of your mother's father Bethuel. Take a wife for yourself there, from among the daughters of Laban, your mother's brother. May God Almighty bless you and make you fruitful and increase your numbers until you become a community of peoples. May he give you and your descendants the blessing given to Abraham, so that you may take possession of the land where you now reside as a foreigner, the land God gave to Abraham." Then Isaac sent Jacob on his way, and he went to Paddan Aram, to Laban son of Bethuel the Aramean, the brother of Rebekah, who was the mother of Jacob and Esau.

Now Esau learned that Isaac had blessed Jacob and had sent him to Paddan Aram to take a wife from there, and that when he blessed him he commanded him, "Do not marry a Canaanite woman," and that Jacob had obeyed his father and mother and had gone to Paddan Aram. Esau then realised how displeasing the Canaanite women were to his father

Isaac; so he went to Ishmael and married Mahalath, the sister of Nebaioth and daughter of Ishmael son of Abraham, in addition to the wives he already had.

It looks like Rebekah's wiles had worked well. She didn't even have to send Jacob away. She had managed to convince Isaac to do her dirty work for her and played on his fears that Jacob would marry an unbeliever. Coincidentally, he did not fear that Jacob might depart the land and not return like his father Abraham had.

Is there a marked cooling of relations between Isaac and Jacob? You couldn't blame Isaac. Jacob had deceived him badly. A father should never be treated with such disrespect as this. Despite this, though, I believe Isaac still cares for Jacob's wellbeing and knows it is true that it would be a huge mistake to take a wife from any of the surrounding tribes. It may well be something which had been on his mind anyway, and now it certainly was an opportune time.

Did Isaac feel sorry for Esau? I'm sure he did. Isaac shared Esau's disappointment and anger, but still, Esau blamed Isaac for the outcome and wanted revenge. He sought to kill his brother, but he did respect his father enough not to do it while his father was still alive, so he was biding his time. In a strange turn of events, Esau shows more respect for his father than Jacob, the chosen one. Isn't it often similar in Churches? How often do we hear it said that Christians are the biggest offenders?

Esau must have been casting around wondering what he could do to express his displeasure and how he could hurt his father, who he thought had hurt him. He figured out that the one thing which was most important to his father was that his sons should marry within the family, so he deliberately went out and married one of Ishmael's daughters.

He was well aware of the bad blood between his father and Ishmael and knew this would hurt his father deeply. It also set up a dangerous situation for himself as his wife would have grown up in bitterness against Isaac, which would feed on Esau's anger. Esau's wife could be counted on to load the shot every opportunity she got and leave Esau, the wild one, to fire the gun.

I am sure that Isaac is very sad at the way things have turned out by this time. It is not how he would have wanted his family to develop, and it is not how he would have brought his family up. I think it is evident by now that the entire family had been undermined by Rebekah, who had continually worked behind her husband's back and favoured Jacob over Esau. Slowly, over time, this had destroyed the family, and now it lay in tatters.

Think of the majority of Churches in the western world these days. There is so much deception and subtility going on that the Church has descended into politics. There is little or no relations with God, and in effect, the organisation has ceased to be a Church.

There is a total disrespect for God, his word, his laws, or his way in many Churches. There is no longer even an attempt to dress things up as a Church, and there is openly a complete abandonment of the idea that there is only one way to be reconciled to God. Everybody can forge their own path.

In the midst of all this, though, God still cares for his Church. He will most certainly punish those who have led his Church astray, but his Church is still dear to him, and he has plans to revive it.

Many who have grown up in the faith will rebel and go their own way. In rebelling, they will deliberately strikeout to offend the Church and the God who nurtured them. It is noticeable and often said that those who have grown up, going to Church when they rebel, go to the most considerable excesses and fall to the lowest depths.

Like Isaac's family, the Church is in complete disarray and has been destroyed by politics. Like Isaac, the Church is merely waiting on death, or in the case of the Church, closure.

CHAPTER 12

Isaac's Death

Isaac's Death
Genesis Ch 35 v 27 – 29
Jacob came home to his father Isaac in Mamre, near Kiriath Arba (that is, Hebron), where Abraham and Isaac had stayed. Isaac lived a hundred and eighty years. Then he breathed his last and died and was gathered to his people, old and full of years. And his sons Esau and Jacob buried him.

A considerable time has passed, much has happened, but the narrative has all been around Jacob and his family. No further mention has been made of Isaac in what must have been around forty years. When we last left Isaac, he was old, blind, and it would appear, no one was even interested in recording what happened to him.

The narrative which made it into the Bible came down the line from Jacob's family, and since they were removed from Isaac, not even the death of Rebekah had been recorded for us. However, Isaac had lived a good number of years after this time, enough to allow Jacob to return with a large family and great riches.

Churches are like this. When they grow older, blind and ineffective, they are predominantly invisible. No one notices them, and nobody is interested in what goes on within their walls. They cease to be a Church and become a club, and the narrative moves to the new Church.

Isaac had passed through his life and carried out his duties, but he had done nothing notable. God had spoken with him and had even made him great promises. God had blessed him beyond that of his father, but Isaac's compromise had left his family in total confusion.

We see a lot of compromise in Churches these days, and the result is always the same, confusion. If there is no discernible difference between the Church and the world, what purpose does the Church serve? The Church is supposed to be the light of the world, but if it is in darkness the same as the world, it cannot light up the world.

This is a sad end to the life of a great man but look around you in your local area. Look at once-proud large Church buildings. What are they now? Bingo halls, cinemas, pubs, dance halls, houses, places of business? A sad end indeed. In the life of Isaac, we have seen a son of promise go through the motions. He has never denied God yet has never given God the proper place in his life.

We see this in many Churches. They proclaim that they believe in God, yet God takes second place to other considerations. Their hearts are not fully committed to the work of the Kingdom. Even those brought up in the Church start to question the point of its existence. They are taught the truth, but it conflicts with what they see the Church doing. The result is total confusion and, ultimately, rejection.

www.ingramcontent.com/pod-product-compliance
Lightning Source LLC
Chambersburg PA
CBHW021159080526
44588CB00008B/424